101 HAIKU

A Journey Through the Seasons

VERA KOCHANOWSKY

Illustrated by

JANINE JOHNSON

101 Haiku: A Journey Through the Seasons

Printed in the United States of America
Cover illustration by Janine Johnson

Luminare Press
442 Charnelton St.
Eugene, OR 97401
www.luminarepress.com

LCCN: 2025909745
ISBN: 979-8-88679-858-6

Days and months are travelers of eternity.
So too are the years that pass by.

—Bashō

CONTENTS

ILLUSTRATIONS

INTRODUCTION

How did this book come to be? Like many other stories, it all started with a journey. Newly retired, my husband and I decided that our first big post-retirement adventure would be a trip to Japan. Our main purpose was to visit an old friend who had also recently retired and moved with his Japanese-born wife to Fukuoka, a large city on the northwestern coast of Kyushu, the southernmost of Japan's four main islands. Had they not made this move, we would never have chosen Japan as our destination.

In past years we had often traveled outside the United States, mainly to Europe, as I have several relatives in Switzerland. But we had never visited Asia before. I expected that Japan would be different from Europe, but I didn't anticipate that it would have such a profound impact on me. I hope to explain in the pages that follow how my two weeks in Japan resulted in an intense fascination with Japanese culture and this surprising outpouring of haiku.

New Horizons: Japanese Culture and Aesthetics

Upon our arrival in Fukuoka, our friends took us to our hotel near the main train station. The hotel was beautiful, and it had everything we needed, and more. The most unusual part of our room was the bathroom. I knew that many Japanese people have a special fondness for bathrooms, and for water in general. Luxuriating in the bath at home, or at a public bath, or at one of the country's many *onsen* (hot springs) is a popular way to relax. But unlike in America, in Japan the bathtub is used exclusively for soaking, not for bathing. So, yes, we had a very nice bathtub, but the shower was strangely affixed to the wall *outside* of the tub. The shower drain consisted of a narrow slit on the floor at the edge of the wall. On the floor under the shower head was a small stool and a large plastic bowl. I was mystified. It seemed a complex system and all the directions were in Japanese, so I struggled a bit with the shower.

But most fascinating and unusual for me was the toilet. Crazy as it sounds, the toilet was the first thing I took a picture of in Japan. Upon lifting the lid, I was immediately confronted with an extensive list of instructions on the underside, again all in Japanese. To the left, mounted on the wall, I found a silvery metal panel of buttons with small cryptic line drawings carved onto each one. During the several days we spent at this hotel, I never felt daring enough to push any of the buttons. However, even without any activation device, the toilet seat would immediately heat up when sat upon. It was my first experience with this luxury, and I missed it when I got home. However, I never got used to another automatic feature of that toilet. While in use, the toilet would play a recording of the sound of rushing water. Probably meant to be soothing as well as masking, this continuous sound of running water troubled me more than it should have. Years of training, reaching back to my childhood, would kick in, and my mind would frantically try to figure out where the water was coming from, so I could go fix the leak and not waste water. How silly! I knew it was only a recording, but subconsciously I could not let go of that overriding feeling of guilt. I was unable to live in the moment and enjoy this aural novelty. My Western mind was getting the better of me.

In Fukuoka and everywhere we traveled, the people we encountered, without exception, were extremely kind and politely solicitous of our welfare and comfort. In the subway trains and on all forms of public transportation, most people (maybe 60-70 percent) wore face masks, showing a concern both for their own health and that of others. The consistency of this gracious demeanor toward everyone, even ignorant tourists, seemed as regular and dependable as the Japanese public transportation system itself. Our American friend, Steve, who can speak Japanese quite well, related to us a difficulty he sometimes encounters in his conversations with native-born Japanese. Their concern with propriety and courteousness would sometimes keep them from "getting to the point" when answering questions. To Western ears, this beating around the bush might seem like a waste of time. I suspect this polished etiquette of words is something instilled quite young, a skill that every civilized, cultured Japanese adult is encouraged to master.

I was struck by how rigorously the Japanese cultivate perfection in all manner of ways. We ate in restaurants daily for lunch and dinner. No matter where we ate, whether in a city or small town, at a tiny or somewhat larger restaurant (there are few very large restaurants in Japan), each dish we ordered came out of the kitchen looking like a work of art. The plates upon which the food was served were beautiful, often locally made, works of art themselves. The food was of the highest quality; we never had a bad meal.

I rarely saw people on the street wearing traditional dress, but everyone was neatly dressed and seemed to be moving purposefully toward their destinations. There were no beggars, no street people;

no one was loitering anywhere. I learned that gun ownership is heavily restricted and that the crime rate in Japan is extremely low. Amazing to me also was the total lack of litter and the extreme rarity of public trash cans. After the sarin terrorist attack in the Tokyo subway in 1995, the government moved to restrict trash cans in all public places. Thirty years later, the people of Japan are now used to stuffing their trash into their purses or pockets until they get home. The only exceptions I noted were recycling bins, which can sometimes be found next to cold drink vending machines.

Another example of the cultivation of perfection is the Japanese garden. We visited several exquisite ones during our stay. But the garden that made the deepest impression on me, and at the same time I believe most exemplified the Japanese ideal, was the garden that surrounds the Adachi Museum of Art in Yasugi. This garden is to be admired from *outside* the garden. Visitors are not permitted to enter the garden itself, but only to look at it from inside the museum. Windows are strategically positioned so that the viewer can get an optimal angle on the outdoor scene. The garden was spectacular. I could not help but marvel at the amount of care that must go into maintaining something of this magnitude and complexity. I watched as gardeners trimmed blades of grass with implements the size of personal hand-held shavers. I did not see, but imagined the tiny rakes that must have been used to shape the fine light-colored gravel, which looked much like sand from a distance, into narrow rows (ocean waves) that surrounded larger black, craggy rocks representing the islands of Japan. How could they do this without disturbing the sand with their feet as they worked? What happens to all this painstaking artistry when a big wind blows through, or a heavy rainstorm? I imagine they must sigh and then begin again.

Another Japanese garden, at Fukuoka's Ohori Park, had a large central lake. As we were walking around it, admiring the rocks, the flowers, and all the greenery, suddenly something amazing happened. Narrow pipes that encircled the entire lake began emitting white mist, and soon the whole area was covered with dense fog. As it dissipated, one could gradually see first the treetops emerge, then the bushes, and finally the grass, rocks, and the lake itself. It was a magical and, for us, a wholly unexpected experience, one created by the mysterious power and properties of water.

Two other examples of traditional arts in Japan that continue to be rigorously cultivated, both intimately tied to water, are *ikebana* (flower arranging) and *chadō* (tea ceremony:"the way of tea"). Unfortunately, I had little exposure to either of these arts during my stay, but I recognize that both reveal much about the Japanese psyche and how it impacts their relationships with others. Both arts exemplify the gift of beauty, the honor and predictability of long-established tradition, and a refined, sincere, yet simple graciousness offered to the viewer or guest.

Regrettably we did not have a chance to see any performances of Kabuki or Noh theater, or traditional Japanese dance. Exposure to traditional music was limited as well, with a couple of exceptions. While visiting the Hakozaki Shrine in Fukuoka, we stumbled upon a group of costumed boys and girls arranged in two rows performing some very athletic *taiko* drumming along with their teacher. Using the full force of their arms and shoulders, each child would play the drum in front of him or her, and then after a few seconds suddenly change places with another drummer to the right or left, or sometimes changing rows. The drumming was quite vigorous, with complex shifting beat patterns. For their second selection the teacher played an ancient-sounding wooden flute while his students continued with their drumming.

Our second experience with traditional music occurred when we visited Yanagawa (which means "willow river"). Because of its many canals retained since the days of the samurai when most people traveled by foot or boat (only high-ranking samurai were permitted to use horses), Yanagawa attracts many tourists who come to enjoy gondola rides through the canals. Willows along the shore offer shade and the many low bridges over the canals are picturesque but sometimes require passengers to duck to avoid hitting their heads. One bridge was so low, our boatman had to jump over it as we floated through underneath. The boatmen, all dressed in traditional costume, use poles to slowly navigate the interconnected waterways while telling colorful stories about the town and its residents. For the last half of the journey the boatmen sing well-known Japanese children's songs written by Hakushū Kitahara (1885-1942), a native son of Yanagawa.

One evening we were dining at the smallest restaurant we encountered in Japan (maximum seating: six!). The owner, a close friend of our hosts, was the cook and the server as well. I asked her about the *samisen,* a three-stringed guitar-like instrument, hanging on the wall. She then graciously agreed to play for us, singing three or four of her own compositions. It was a charming experience I will not soon forget. Here, like at most every other dining establishment we visited, we were graciously received and treated to a unique and rewarding aesthetic and culinary experience.

Japan's Religions and Foreign Influence

As a major port city and the closest commercial center to Korea and China, Fukuoka holds great significance as the primary site where art, learning, and culture were transmitted to Japan from the mainland. It was here where two major Mongolian invasions were attempted in the late thirteenth century (in 1274 and again in 1281). The failure of Kublai Khan's (1215-1294) massive forces to conquer Japan is attributed to divine intervention. In both cases a devastating typhoon ("divine wind" or *kamikaze*) caused the catastrophic ruin of the Mongolian fleet. Japan's victory was celebrated, and in the ensuing centuries much was done to preserve Japan's integrity against other potential outside invaders. Isolationism eventually intensified and strict rules against all kinds of foreign influence were imposed for more than 250 years, from the late sixteenth until the mid-nineteenth century. Trade with other countries was severely restricted. From Europe, only Dutch traders were permitted inside the country during this period, and they were restricted to Dejima, a small island off the coast of Nagasaki. Seen as a threat to the shogunate authority, the practice of Christianity was also outlawed. Religious intolerance intensified, as exemplified by the public crucifixion of twenty-six Japanese and foreign Christians in a public square in Nagasaki in 1597, and continued until Christianity was legalized after the Meiji Restoration (1873).

Even before the Mongolian invasions took place, Japan's culture was shaped by Korean and Chinese influence. This can be seen in many areas, including art, architecture, poetry, ceramics, painting, writing system (Chinese characters), philosophy, social ethics, technology (e.g., fireworks), rice cultivation, dress, and religion. While the Shinto religion was indigenous to Japan, with some form of it existing since prehistoric times, it was not until the sixth century CE that Buddhism was brought to Japan from China through Korea. The two religions were accepted and combined by the Japanese, a practice called *shimbutsu-shūgō* (the syncretism of Shinto and Buddhism). Shinto shrines and Buddhist temples were often built side by side, and people would (and still do) visit and worship at both on the same day. Once Christianity was legalized in Japan, its practices and dedicated spaces (churches, cathedrals, and chapels) were readily incorporated into the lives of the Japanese people.

This all-encompassing embrace of different religions is something that struck me as uniquely Japanese. In my experience, it is relatively unusual for an American to combine different religions and religious practices. Indeed, in some communities it is thought strange or even blasphemous to attend a religious service outside of one's own denomination. Not so in Japan where it is not uncommon for a betrothed couple to seek a blessing for their union at a Shinto shrine, get married in a Christian chapel, and visit departed family members at a Buddhist cemetery.

Shinto shrines are dedicated to *kami* (a specific god or gods), and the person seeking a blessing or the fulfillment of a wish may choose one or another shrine depending on the special power associated with the deity celebrated at that shrine. Buddhist temples are generally dedicated to the Buddha or to a small number of Buddhist deities (Bodhisattvas: enlightened beings). There are tens of thousands of shrines and Buddhist temples throughout Japan, some large, some small. Some are considered so important that every Japanese, no matter where they reside in Japan, will try to visit them at least once in their lives.

During our stay we visited numerous Shinto shrines and Buddhist temples. Some, like the Yūtoku Inari Shrine and the Itsukushima (floating) Shrine are world famous and attract huge numbers of visitors annually. We also saw some lesser-known religious sites tucked away in various neighborhoods. Each was a world unto itself, a place to retreat from the noisy modern world and meditate, admire nature, contemplate relics or religious statuary, pray, make a wish, or receive a blessing. People of all ages, of all income levels, come and go freely, spending as much or as little time as they wish. Other than occasional drumming and bell ringing, a quiet atmosphere is generally maintained. These sacred places offer everyone the opportunity to contemplate and commune with long-standing Japanese religious tradition, culture, and aesthetics in a garden-like setting. Impressive large religious statuary we saw included the Reclining Buddha at the Nanzoin Temple in Sasaguri and a hillside Kannon in Nagasaki.

Post Journey: Discovering Japanese Literature

After a busy, fascinating two weeks of travel in Japan, it was finally time to say goodbye to our friends Steve and Yukari. By this time my interest in Japanese culture had grown so much that I decided to continue my study of it. I had brought along to Japan a guidebook which mentioned a work considered to be a masterpiece of Japanese literature, *The Narrow Road to the Deep North* by Matsuo Bashō (1644-1694). I resolved to read it as soon as I could find an English translation. After returning home, I did just that and discovered Bashō's significant role in establishing haiku as an independent poetic form.

Haiku arose from two earlier poetic forms: (1) *waka* (or *tanka*) having five lines of thirty-one syllables (5-7-5-7-7) and (2) linked verse (*renga*). Originally a courtly art form, linked verse was eventually adopted by the middle class too. It remained very popular in Japan for a long time. A kind of spontaneous social game involving two or more competing poets, it had very elaborate rules. It always started with a *hokku*, a verse consisting of 5-7-5 syllables, which was often composed by a special guest of honor, perhaps a famous visiting poet like Bashō. Next a "flank" verse of 7-7 syllables would be added, usually by another poet. These two structures would continue in alternation for 36, or sometimes as many as 100 verses or more. The *hokku* eventually broke off from linked verse, as did the first three lines of the *waka*, to become the independent haiku form (5-7-5) we know today.

I noted that English translations of Japanese haiku tend to be rendered in three lines even though the original Japanese text is often written in a single line. In translation it is not always possible to stick with seventeen syllables or with a 5-7-5 syllable structure and still have a faithful translation of the Japanese text. Unlike English, Japanese does not have stressed and unstressed syllables, so poetic meter is not apparent. Although line-ending rhyme is not a feature of Japanese haiku, one does find expressive use of alliteration and assonance. Japanese authors were sensitive to the sound of the words they chose and to the length of the words themselves. For example, using several single-syllable words in a row instead of one or two double- or triple-syllable words creates a different effect. These two elements (word length and the color or timbre of the words) were used by poets to help support the images they were trying to create.

I continued my study of classical haiku by reading translations of other works by Bashō and poetry by other important Japanese poets including Yosa Buson (1716-1783), Kobayashi Issa (1763-1828), Masaoka Shiki (1867-1902), and several of their contemporaries. This deep immersion into traditional Japanese poetry helped keep me in "traveler" mode, and I found I was learning new things about Japan while reinforcing what I had already observed firsthand about the societal values, and the aesthetic and religious dimensions of Japanese culture.

I found Bashō an especially intriguing and inspiring figure. Even though his oeuvre is smaller than that of some later Japanese poets such as Issa or Shiki, we are fortunate to also have Bashō's many comments on how to write haiku, or *haikai* as it was then called. Because I found his instructions so helpful, I will discuss some of his most profound thoughts and insights below, while also giving a few examples of his poetry.

The Power of the Seasons

A crucial element in classical haiku is an intentional reference to a season, either the name of the season itself (spring, summer, winter, autumn), or something that is traditionally associated with a particular season, sometimes called a seasonal word (e.g. cherry blossoms=spring; the moon=autumn). Here Bashō states in no uncertain terms how important nature and the seasons should be to the poet:

> It is the poetic spirit that leads one to follow nature and become a friend with things of the seasons. For a person who has the spirit, everything he sees becomes a flower, and everything he imagines turns into a moon. Those who do not see the flower are no different from barbarians, and those who do not imagine the moon are akin to beasts. Leave barbarians and beasts behind; follow nature and return to nature.[1]

It is easy to see how the beauties of nature can be a great source of inspiration to any poet. But there is more to it than that. Why do the seasons and nature hold such significance for Bashō? The seasons show the *permanence of impermanence*. All things change

1 Robert Hass, *The Essential Haiku: Versions of Bashō, Buson, and Issa*, Hopewell, NJ: The Ecco Press, 1994, p 237.

and continue to change. This overarching truth impacts everyone and everything. Nature shows this continuum of change in a physical way. We see the beauty of the cherry blossoms in spring and know that the wind will soon sweep them away, but we still enjoy them, and perhaps revere them more *because* they are transitory. We also recognize that they will one day return, even if we are not here to see them. It allows us to focus on the transcendent beauty and significance of every moment and every aspect of nature, whether lasting or fleeting, each equally worthy of reflection.

All divisions of time—seconds, minutes, hours, days, weeks, months, and even the seasons—are artificial to a certain degree. Time itself is seamless; one moment inevitably bleeds into the next, and all moments are intimately connected to each other in our consciousness. Even in sleep, which normally divides our days, our minds continue to review past events and attempt to imagine the future. As we progress through the year and mark our calendars with appointments, holidays, and other events, we are always processing what has happened to us in the past and what might be coming. All of time is connected; it is an ongoing continuum.

Haiku: A Poetry of Simple, Ordinary Things

The older *waka* poetry, with its courtly roots, was concerned with beauty. But haiku had different aims. Bashō says one must open oneself to the common world. Two brief quotes of his follow:

> The bones of haikai are plainness and oddness.
>
> Eat vegetable soup rather than duck stew.[2]

This does not mean there can be no beauty in haiku, but rather that one should not shrink away from describing exactly what one sees, whether it is beautiful or ugly. The depiction of ordinary sights and events has universal appeal. Everyone, wealthy or poor, young or old, will be able to relate to them. Many haiku are simply descriptions of what the poet sees. The art comes in showing the object's significance within the context of its surroundings, its time and place. Haiku is a poetry of things, of reality. We live in a world of things, and we must find a way to relate to them and understand them, so that we can better understand ourselves. If you can see yourself in everything, then everything is in you, and all things become one. Bashō says:

2 Hass, p. 238.

> Every form of insentient existence—plants, stones, or utensils—has its individual feelings similar to those of men.[3]

Granted, this requires a bit of imagination! If you can view and describe the world as a child would—simply, directly, with a minimum of intellectualizing, this is close to an optimal haiku viewpoint. Children love to play, to make believe, and readily give life to lifeless things. Indeed, Shiki, who was much influenced by Buson, writes about the necessity of combining fantasy with realism.[4] Too much detail, too many rational explanations can ruin fantasy. In Bashō's words, "Is there any good in saying everything?"[5] Young children will state the obvious simply and artlessly, and the emotions they feel, joy just as much as sorrow, are raw, sincere, and intense. Everything is new to them, every experience a fresh awakening. Haiku requires you to open all your senses to the world fearlessly, as a child would, and receive what the world offers each day.

Many haiku are light and even humorous (strongly humorous or satirical haiku are called *senryu*), while others are tinged with a wistful sadness or loneliness. It is remarkable to me how the great haiku poets can

---

3 Hass, p. 237.

4 Hiroaki Sato, *On Haiku,* New York: New Directions Publishing Co., 2018, p. 151.

5 Hass, p. 234.

do so much with so few words and just one or two images. Significance is there, lightly suggested, like a simple line drawing. Blyth says:

> A haiku is not a poem, it is not literature, it is a hand beckoning, a door half-opened, a mirror wiped clean.[6]

Religion and Other Influences on Japanese Haiku

We know that Bashō was a student of Zen and that he may have studied with the priest Butcho.[7] His poetry and his teaching reflect Zen influence. But while haiku is often linked with Zen Buddhism, there is something of Shinto in it too. Shinto focuses on the worship of ancestors and the natural world, including the changing seasons. The gods are everywhere and in everything. In every plant, animal, rock, season, person, sound, in everything there is a god. According to Japanese legend there are 8 million Shinto gods, a number interpreted as being uncountable or infinite. There is a god in everything, and so too, according

6 Reginald Horace Blyth, *Haiku, vol. 1,* Brooklyn, NY: Angelico Press, 2021, p. 272.

7 Matsuo Bashō, *The Narrow Road to the Deep North and Other Travel Sketches* (trans. by Nobuyuki Yuasa), New York: Penguin Books, 1966, p. 27.

to Bashō, can everything be the subject of a haiku.[8]

Buddhism, as mentioned above, ideally guides the art of haiku. Some shared concepts include:

1. The supremacy of the moment, all of life is in this moment
2. Life consists of constant change, all things are transient
3. The interconnectivity of everything in the universe
4. Focus on simplicity and naturalness
5. The cultivation of a tranquil mind to better understand the world
6. Reverence for all animate and even inanimate things, which leads to compassion toward all, including oneself

Like Buddhism, early Chinese poetry had a strong impact on classical Japanese haiku poets. In reading a collection of old Chinese verse (most of it written 700-900 CE), I discovered that depictions of nature were often used to establish the mood of the poem. No doubt this powerful connection to nature in early

8 Kenneth Yasuda, *The Japanese Haiku*. Rutland VT: Tuttle Publishing, 1957, p. 15.

Chinese verse influenced Japanese poets. We know that Bashō read and admired the works of Du Fu (712-770) and Li Po (701-762), among others.[9]

Bashō: The Traveling Poet

During the last decade of his life, Bashō undertook several journeys. By this time, he had made a name for himself and was much revered. In the years just preceding his journeys, he had become somewhat isolated, living alone and relying on the generosity of friends and students for his very survival. One admirer had even built him a house in 1680, but two years later it burned down. A year later another house was built for him, but he soon decided to leave and begin the first of his extended journeys.

Traveling in those days was a dangerous and costly undertaking, especially challenging for those with little means. Wherever he went, Bashō continued to rely on friends, disciples, priests, and admirers for sustenance and shelter. Often one of his trusted disciples would accompany him, functioning as a servant and traveling companion. But why, at this point in his life, did he decide to subject himself to such strain and hardship? Bashō explains:

9 William Scott Wilson, *A Beginner's Guide to Japanese Haiku*, Rutland, VT: Tuttle Publishing, 2022, p. 25.

> Since ancient times, those with a feeling for poetry did not mind carrying knapsacks on their backs or putting straw sandals on their feet or wearing simple hats that barely protected them from the elements. They took delight in disciplining their minds through hardship and thereby attaining a knowledge of the true nature of things.[10]

In his opening phrase, Bashō may be recalling the Chinese poet Li Po who famously wandered for many years, or Iio Sogi (1421-1502) who roamed Japan lecturing and teaching during the last decades of his life.[11] Sogi died on the road, as Bashō would as well. Bashō believed that hardship—cold, hunger, living in poverty—would make him a better poet. He was right. With these journeys he brought the *haibun* (a literary form that combines prose and poetry) to its greatest height. These accounts of his last travels are considered his best works today. His experiences on these journeys, during which he would see new sights daily, visit people and historic places, including famous temples and the sites of ancient battles, would indeed help him discipline his mind and hone his craft.[12] By seeing things with his own eyes and reflecting on them, he grew to become one with his

10 Hass, pp. 237-238.

11 Wilson, p. 82.

12 Hass, p. x.

country. Buson and Issa, perhaps inspired by Bashō, wandered for many years too. In 1778 Buson, also a talented painter, illustrated Bashō's masterpiece, *The Narrow Road to the Deep North.*

In the autumn of 1694, Bashō was traveling near Osaka when he fell ill. Mukai Kyorai (1651-1704), one of Bashō's disciples, was with him and witnessed Bashō's last poetic effort, his "death verse." He died four days later.[13]

Ill on a journey;
My dreams wander
Over a withered moor.[14]

Kyorai would later write the *Kyoraisho,* which details events in Bashō's life and his teachings. He remained at Bashō's bedside along with Takarai Kikaku (1661-1707) during Bashō's last illness.[15]

Bashō: The Teacher

One central principle of haiku is that it should represent life. Here follows a revealing exchange between Bashō and one of his students, Kikaku. Kikaku had written a poem about a dragonfly and wanted his master's reaction.

13 Bashō (Yuasa), p. 47.
14 Blyth, vol. 4, p. 288.
15 Wilson, p.187.

Take a pair of wings
From a dragonfly, you would
Make a pepper-pod.

Bashō insisted that this poem was not haiku because it would be necessary to kill the dragonfly to give away his wings. He suggested instead:

Add a pair of wings
To a pepper-pod, you would
Make a dragonfly.[16]

A contrarian to my bones, my mind immediately asks: Where does this pair of wings come from? Who will be missing them? But the point I think Bashō is making is this: haiku should reflect the wonder and diversity of life, rather than senseless destruction.

Here follows what has long been considered Bashō's most famous poem. He composed it one spring day in the company of several students. There was light rain falling and the river was close by. They could hear frogs jumping into the water. Bashō shared the last line of his poem, and one student suggested an opening which referred to a flowering yellow rose.[17] But Bashō ultimately decided on:

16 Kenneth Yasuda, *A Pepper Pod*, New York: Alfred A. Knopf, 1947, p. ii.
17 Bashō (Yuasa), p.32.

Old pond;
A frog jumps in—
The sound of water.[18]

This poem has been analyzed by a multitude of authors, but I hope you'll forgive me if I add my own thoughts here. Why is this considered a masterful poem? There are several elements worth pointing out. The scene is set with something ancient, something that has been there for eons, unmoving, quiet, and perhaps dark and stagnant, covered with scum. Then a living being is introduced, something slimy, shiny and quick, that pauses at the edge of this ancient monument. Suddenly we have several examples of discord: The silence is broken by the sound of the frog jumping in. The still water is visibly broken up by the frog, perhaps with a few residual ripples remaining for a time. The living thing momentarily disturbs the process of decay in the old pond, the living and the dead interact in that instant and become one thing. Between the visible and the audible, it is the audible, the sound of water, that is emphasized. The deep resonant "kerplop" made by the frog represents the vibrancy of life which outstrips the silence and decay of the pond with its energy.

Delving further into Bashō's insistence on following nature, I found the following passage most instructive and inspiring. It explains the importance

18 Blyth, vol. 2, p. 253.

of becoming one with your subject, an essential step toward enlightened expression.

> Go to the pine if you want to learn about the pine, or to the bamboo if you want to learn about the bamboo.[19] And in doing so, you must leave your subjective preoccupation with yourself. Otherwise, you impose yourself on the object and do not learn. Your poetry issues of its own accord when you and the object have become one—when you have plunged deeply enough into the object to see something like a hidden glimmering there. However well phrased your poetry may be, if your feeling is not natural—if the object and you are separate—then your poetry is not true poetry but merely your subjective counterfeit.[20]

Bashō: The Human Being

Shortly after beginning the first of his long journeys (recounted in his *The Records of a Weather-Exposed Skeleton*), Bashō encounters a small crying child, apparently abandoned by his parents. His heart goes out to the little boy with pity, and he writes:

19 The pine is the symbol for longevity and steadfastness; bamboo represents someone who can adapt to changing circumstances without breaking.

20 Bashō (Yuasa), p 33.

> As we walked along the Fuji River, we came upon an abandoned child, about two years of age and crying pathetically. I wondered if its parents, finding the waves of this floating world as uncontrollable as the river, had abandoned him there, thinking his life would last only as long as the dew. The child looked as fragile as bush clover petals in the wind. I took some food from my sleeve and gave it to the child as we passed.[21]

Here follows the poem Bashō composed to commemorate this encounter:

The ancient poet
Who pitied monkeys for their cries,
What would he say, if he saw
This child crying in the autumn wind?[22]

Although he was determined to begin his journey to the north in the early spring of 1689, it was not without regret that Bashō left his friends behind:

Birds mourn,
Fishes weep
With tearful eyes.[23]

21 Hass, p. 15.
22 Bashō (Yuasa), p. 52.
23 Bashō (Yuasa), p. 98.

Bashō was feeling his age late in life when he wrote:

This autumn—
Why am I growing old?
Bird disappearing among clouds.[24]

Initially distracted by his growing frailty, Bashō then turns his eyes to the sky and to nature, his muse, and perhaps wonders: Where has that bird gone? Maybe there is something wondrous behind the clouds, or maybe there is nothing. Or perhaps Bashō sees himself as the bird, soon to be obscured by a cloud. This haiku reminds me of two by Issa, the second composed after the death of his young daughter.

A world of grief and pain:
Flowers bloom
Even then.[25]

This world of dew
is only a world of dew—
and yet[26]

24 Hass, p. 53.
25 Blyth, vol. 1, p. 177.
26 *The Sound of Water: Haiku by Bashō, Buson, Issa, and other poets*, trans. by Sam Hamill. Boston: Shambhala Publications, 2000, p. xix.

Bashō and the Banana Tree

One of his students gave Bashō a banana sapling in the winter of 1680. It thrived in his garden, and he came to admire it so much that he adopted Bashō (banana tree) as his pen name from then on. What elevated the banana tree to such heights in his opinion? He noted that its leaves were easily torn by the wind and the rain, its flowers were not at all beautiful, nor was its wood of any use to a builder.

> I love the tree, however, for its very uselessness... I sit underneath it, and enjoy the wind and rain that blow against it.[27]

The tree was *useless* in almost every way, yet Bashō loved it. He admired its dramatic shape, its extreme responsiveness to the elements, the shade and protection it afforded, and probably also the way it thrived under his care. There is something in that simple relationship that naturally leads to poetry and yet goes beyond poetry: man to tree; tree to nature; nature to universe.

Writing Haiku Today: A Mosaic of Life

After reading the works of Bashō and other classical Japanese haiku poets in English translation, I was

27 Bashō (Yuasa), pp. 25-26.

curious to find out how haiku evolved subsequently, and particularly how English-speaking poets are handling the form today. Searching online, I came across the websites of three American haiku associations, The Haiku Society of America, The Haiku Foundation, and Modern Haiku. Each had plentiful examples of haiku written by their members. Based on what I found on these websites, it is clear that traditional rules have relaxed quite a bit over time. Most, although not all, contemporary haiku are still written in three lines. However, they rarely adhere to the traditional 5-7-5 format of seventeen syllables. Most are quite a bit shorter, some having as few as ten syllables. Capitalization and punctuation are practically non-existent. Seasonal references sometimes appear but are no longer required. The goal seems to be to pare things down as much as possible, leaving a great deal to the reader's imagination. Haiku has always been a short poetic form, but its structure today has become much more flexible.

In our modern life we are rarely encouraged to observe little things. Although we may look at our surroundings (when our eyes are not glued to our cell phones), we often don't see what is really there. We don't take the time to make those connections that fill our world, and which can bring us a clearer understanding of ourselves and our relationship to all that exists, one little piece at a time. Haiku can be a form of meditation, a focus on a particular object or experience that has elicited a feeling or even just some kind of response in us, a spark of recognition, a connection to something we have known or experienced before. Each of these moments of understanding becomes a tiny piece of beauty in the mosaic of our lives.

As with most arts, cultivating a haiku mind frame takes some practice, but once you've succeeded, inspiration and inclination tend to increase. I find developing this mindset akin to trying to remember your dreams. The more you do it, the easier it becomes. I've come to the point now where I can recognize a haiku moment as it is happening. When I am really "in tune" with my surroundings I can come up with many more haiku than when I am distracted.

Expressing a haiku moment through poetry, or through any form of writing, allows us both to remember it more clearly and to share that experience with others. But one might find a good subject yet have no idea how to express it in words. The "artificial" structure of classical haiku (5-7-5 syllables) gives us a starting point, a framework for our thoughts. The extreme brevity of the form may seem like an insurmountable barrier to clear and effective expression. However, it also does something very positive. It forces the poet to economize, to whittle the idea down to its most essential elements. Stripped of everything unnecessary, the resulting poem usually becomes both more powerful and more accessible, inviting the pliable mind of the reader to take it, and run with it.

The idea of "less is more" is nothing new. In art and music there are plenty of examples. The human mind enjoys and even revels in these intentional gaps. A good art teacher will tell you that when you draw an object or a person you can leave certain things out. Some lines can and should be lighter, and some can be left out altogether. Dark areas enhance the lighter spaces, and vice versa. Knowing what to minimize or leave out is where the artist shows his or her mastery. The viewer's mind must fill in these gaps. It regularly does so with surprisingly little effort.

In music the blank or light space is silence. The musician's canvas is time. Our minds always compare the present moment to what has just been heard. The impact of what will come is shaped by what is played or not played in this moment. One can get used to loud sounds if the ear is bombarded with them continually. But if there is a moment of silence just before it, a loud cymbal crash will have a more startling impact. The best musicians know how to use silence, the spaces between notes, to move their listeners.

Pulitzer Prize winning poet Henry Taylor (1942-2024), who grew up in the Virginia countryside, compared "the wordless communication between a horse and its rider" to the art of poetry when he said, "Poetry is sometimes in the words you have not been able to say or write down, but somehow need to suggest in the words that are there."[28] The words a poet chooses will, of course, impact any unwritten implication. In true works of art, the empty space, silence, or implied missing words will elevate the meaning and power of the composition. Artists in any medium would do well to study the mysterious and fertile realm that lies between the concrete and the subtly suggested.

When we argue our point, sometimes it seems like the more we talk, the less we convince. By over-explaining we show a kind of weakness. Sometimes, a non-verbal example speaks louder than words. Sometimes only a word or two is necessary. Although it may seem contradictory, perhaps with fewer words we can get closer to our goal.

About These Haiku

As I began writing haiku, I was guided more by the spirit and style of the classical Japanese poets, rather than by the modern trends I later encountered. I took Bashō's instructions to heart and tried to discover my own voice within the confines of this tiny form. Of course, because of my background, I realize that I speak haiku with a distinctly Western accent; and, as a

28 Harrison Smith, "Pulitzer-winning formalist poet with an eye on rural life," *The Washington Post,* November 24, 2024, C4.

child of my time, I have also quite naturally let modern references creep in. My focus throughout this experience has been to try to pack as much significance into seventeen syllables as I possibly could. This often led to denser, more complex results than generally found in both modern and even most classical haiku.

Many of the haiku in this volume follow the traditional 5-7-5 syllable pattern; others have seventeen syllables but with lines of varying syllable counts. A few poems are longer, a few shorter than seventeen syllables. I tried to be flexible and let the poem tell me how to punctuate and distribute the syllables over two to five lines. I find punctuation often contributes to meaning, but I realize that exerting too much control may impede the reader's imagination. I have tried to strike a balance between clarity and suggestion.

These haiku were written as they came to me, not in this order. After completing all of them, I arranged them in seasonal order, an organization frequently found in classical Japanese anthologies. In addition to arranging them by season, I also attempted to follow an important principle of classic Japanese linked verse. I tried to apply Bashō's concept of *nioizuke* (linked by scent) in which "one verse carries the atmosphere of its predecessor much as the fragrance of a flower is carried by the wind."[29] Abrupt shifts of mood and theme were considered highly desirable in

29 Wilson, p. 187.

linked verse, but there had to be a subtle link between each verse too, the more subtle the better.

Some of the links in this collection are subtle, while others are more obvious. However, there will always be some kind of connection between one poem and the next. My goal in doing this was not to mimic traditional linked verse, but to create an overarching continuity for this collection of poems. I wanted to paint a portrait of a year, this particular year, with a parade of images reflecting my experiences and thoughts. What more wondrous a canvas could we as word painters ask for, than one as rich and grounding as the seasons of the year?

We are always learning and growing. While perfection remains a distant star, this new way of seeing, thinking, and formulating my ideas has brought me to a new plane. I have Japan, Bashō, and "the sound of water" to thank for helping me and my Western mind rise to the challenge.

ACKNOWLEDGEMENTS

First and foremost, I want to thank our dear friends Steven and Yukari Lassagne who were our hosts and tour guides in Japan. They put great effort into planning and arranging our trip and accompanied us everywhere. Yukari, who is an expert chef, selected the restaurants where we dined, and cooked us a wonderful Japanese-style meal in her own kitchen on our last night. Obviously, this book would never have seen the light of day without their generosity and willingness to take us by the hand and show us around.

On our way back to Virginia, we stopped in the San Francisco Bay Area to visit some friends. We met up with one longtime friend, Sally Freyberg, who has always been very supportive of my writing projects. Whenever I hear from Sally, she regularly asks, "What are you working on next?" After this visit, Sally sent me an email in which she suggested that I try writing just a little each day, to get into the habit again. Since I was reading and learning about haiku at the time, I thought that maybe I could indeed write one haiku a day. So that's how I got started. I have Sally to thank for the suggestion, for her encouragement, as well as for reading through them, a few at a time as I was composing them, and sharing her impressions.

Before we left for Japan, my friend Lucy Whitley lent me an excellent guidebook on Japan which I read thoroughly before we left. It referred to Bashō's *The Narrow Road to the Deep North* which got me started on my haiku investigations.

I am heavily indebted to Janine Johnson for her contribution to this project. Once I completed the haiku for this book, I sent them to her in hopes that she might agree to design a cover and, if she felt inclined, to illustrate some of the poems. I was overjoyed when I received her packet of drawings. I first met Janine in the late 1980s, when I was a graduate student at Stanford University. Before finishing my degree, I decided to commission a double manual harpsichord from the renowned Berkeley builder John Phillips. In the process, I was introduced to Janine, the artist who decorated all of John's instruments. We got along well, and after looking at samples of her work I knew she would do a marvelous job on my instrument (she did!). Ten years later, the decoration she designed and executed on a second instrument I ordered from John was equally remarkable. I was familiar with her Chinese-style decorations and knew she had a knack for creating fanciful figures, animals, birds, and landscapes. Her consummate artistic skill, her imagination, and her previous experience with Asian art styles, made her uniquely suited to this project.

As with my previous books, I have found it a crucial step in the process of preparing a book for publication to gather feedback from trusted friends. My deep thanks go to the following people for their help in reviewing earlier versions of this book: Jenneke Fijn van Draat, Sally Freyberg, Ruth van Baak Griffioen, Marian Gormley, Judy Ikels, Marion Jetton, Janine Johnson, Kathryn Korfonta, Thomas Kramer, Steven Lassagne, Misato Miyamasu, and Marsha Scialdo.

Lastly, I'd like to thank my husband, Gregory Hutton, for his help and support on this project (and for taking this trip with me!), and with all the other projects, large and small, I've undertaken during the forty plus years of our marriage. Arigato!

101 HAIKU

A Journey Through the Seasons

Haiku:
an instant captured,
framed like a picture
with words from the heart.

Listen to Bashō!
Standing pine, waving bamboo:
wisest of teachers.

Stubbornly snowdrops
push their little heads against
roofs of crusty frost.

White cherry blossoms
do not recall winter snowflakes
soundlessly falling.

As dawn awakens,
gray light holds all in stillness,
reflections frozen.

Each day's breaking dawn
offers mystery and hope.
Those who see it smile.

Broad frozen river
bellows and groans in pain as
spring returns once more.

Gray metal guardrail
frigid and icy as the
brook flowing beneath.

Following the stream
as far as we can,
my friend and I together.

Spring's warming sunshine
beneath clear rushing waters
turns stones into gold.

Rainy April day:
the road writhes, covered with worms.
Earth's life spills over.

Invisible cloak—
all alone in the dappled
undergrowth, a fawn.

A bird sings above,
never tiring of his message:
"I am here right now."

My mind's aflutter,
it won't sit still,
now is already tomorrow.

Pushed roughly along
by the reckless winds of May—
Where are we going?

Where will it stop,
the water from my tap?
No traveler can say.

Japan in May

Fourteen Haiku

The sound of water
plays in the hotel's bathroom:
odd pangs of guilt.

Cranes in rice paddies
standing in muddy water—
Waiting for a fish?

Japanese garden:
no blade of grass out of place,
perfect waves of sand.

Parasol shaded,
a kimono-clad lady
enjoys irises.

Visiting the Kushida Shrine

Two wise stone lions
proudly stand beside the gate.
One speaks, one listens.

Taiko drumming sounds
as paper fortunes flutter.
Old tree takes it in.

My fortune is good!
"Like boats gathering at the port."
Just 100 yen.

A Boat Ride in Yanagawa

In the heat of day
our boat glides under bridges
and rustling willows.

Oohs and aahs ring out
as we pass the childhood home
of Yoko Ono.

The old boatman croons
many treasured childhood songs.
Passengers all smile.

Gunkanjima:
shining island!
Hive of productivity,
crumbling slowly
into the sea.

Twenty-six were killed
on a gentle rise of hill,
now deeply honored.

Unperturbed, Kannon
stands on a tortoise's back
gazing on tombstones.

His last day on earth,
the Great Buddha lies serene,
young as a sunrise.

Waveless and silent,
the lake's dark surface reflects
sunlight brilliantly.

How calmly the stream
creeps by, wavelessly flowing
to the stormy sea.

The sea tastes the shore
again and again.
It can never get its fill.

Through a telescope
I see waves cross a distant lake,
heat rise off the land.

A brook sings as it
frolics amongst rocks and stones:
children's laughter.

Revolving door:
a child's delight!
Who goes in might,
or might not,
come out.

At the playground,
a child on the rusty swing:
the cawing of crows.

Birds must sing louder
when the gardener arrives
with his leaf blower.

Confounded, the winds!
East wind blowing from the west,
the west from the east.

A sweet passing breeze
awakens the garden chimes
to new enchantments.

When we are apart
my mind curls up in your arms,
our hearts beat as one.

A gentle darkness:
evening of a summer's day,
below, the warm earth.

A lush June garden
in dimming day is lit by
a single firefly.

Even garden weeds
when rudely uprooted
offer Earth's sweet scent.

Through the dewy grass
a cat creeps, delicately
lifting up each paw.

A red fox trots by,
just minding his own business.
Many eyes widen.

Will he stay or run?
Frozen, bright eyes unblinking,
a startled rabbit.

The bull does not care,
trampling the rose without thought.
But thorns don't forget.

Climbing ivy,
most ambitious of creepers.
Final stop: the Sun.

Lush forest enfolds
a dead tree,
bare, deeply creased:
an ancient temple.

Quick-growing green vines
decorate the edges of
a new parking lot.

Summer's bounty—
There's no room in the garden
for any more weeds.

"It's too hot, too hot,"
sighs the humid summer air.
"It's too hot to move."

Late August drought:
just a few drops of rain and
Earth sighs with relief.

Rapturous drunkenness:
the fragrance of mimosa
hanging in the air.

High on this mountain
the silence is deafening.
A tiny bug hums.

Dark mountains of cloud
boil up in the western sky:
ominous brooding.

A restless night:
roaring thunder, driving rain,
then the songs of birds.

Silly umbrellas!
Blown inside out by the wind.
Holding up the rain?

Well, well, here we are,
my brain and I,
sitting around
thinking silly thoughts.

Even great poets
write bad poems sometimes.

The mind, a blank page,
waiting for a drop of ink
to appear, like dew.

A shimmer of blue
clings to a wispy pine:
dreaming dragonfly.

Morning glory
opens her alluring eye,
but soon goes back to sleep.

Timidly the Moon
checks her face in a clear lake:
autumn's glowing night.

Just a hint of chill—
The sound of crickets growing
in autumn moonlight.

When do worries die?
Pushed down by brief distractions,
just to rise again.

Fear runs with quick feet
(with quicker ones at night)
but has nowhere to go.

Complaining mother,
daughter answers with complaints,
complaining mother.

I was born a girl,
to my father's great chagrin.
No one is perfect.

Nature and mankind
never quite see eye to eye.
That's human nature.

When worry steals the show
all day, all night, every hour,
peace loses interest.

Your voice, so soothing,
like warm butter over grits.
Let me not forget.

See "For Robert" in the Appendix.

Faithful practice:
opera singer's daily drills,
her dog joins in too.

Hidden, a green frog
rests on fallen leaves,
croaking deep profundity.

Someone spilled paint
all over the fall mountains—
each leaf, a masterpiece.

As mists of fall rise,
last night's raindrop trickles down
a turning leaf's cheek.

Flaming sunsets draw
the eyes of young and old,
but cool in evening wind.

An evening shadow:
a vole scampers to my door,
turns and darts away.

Poor jack-o-lantern
awoke with a hole in his head!
The squirrel was hungry.

How do they do it?
They must have eyes in hidden places:
geese in flight.

A gifted cricket
sings a glorious concert
down in the basement.

A mouse stirs above
with relentless scritch, scratch, scritch—
Sleep scurries away.

Brittle brown leaves fly
through the garden and stop to
chatter at my door.

Dew now turned to frost
crunches loudly underfoot:
winter's new carpet.

Woven masterpiece:
the enormous, tangled roots
of an ancient tree.

My grandmother's clock
ticked so loudly without stop,
I can still hear it.

Suddenly alone,
years of marriage have flown by,
each day now too long.

The white winter Moon
shines too brightly as the year's
last days slip away.

How lonely the snow—
hidden, the whole world beneath,
above, blankets of cloud.

A scarecrow watches
over empty snowy fields,
hatless and headless.

When a child suffers,
no matter what the reason,
a parent's heart cries.

Bound by chains of love
to my dying mother's bed,
age weighs on us both.

O how long the road,
solitary traveler!
A friend shortens it.

Nothing so friendly—
the smell of coffee brewing
in a warm kitchen.

Tip—tip tap tip tap!
Winter sleet falls on the roof:
urgent messaging.

Whirling and churning,
cutting through the black of night:
winter's first snowfall.

Cold night in the woods,
sparks fly up from the campfire
to mingle with stars.

I am reminded
by each glorious sunset:
all things are fleeting.

Childhood days long gone,
linger in the evening mist
and play in my dreams.

Baby's mother sings
a little lullaby.
Each breath brings them peace.

NOTES ON HAIKU

Each day's breaking dawn (p. 49):
Inspired by the film *Perfect Days*.

Visiting the Kushida Shrine (p. 58):
One of Fukuoka's oldest shrines, the Kushida Shrine was founded in 757 CE.

Two lion-dogs (*komainu*) are often placed on either side of the main gate at Shinto shrines. They are there to keep evil spirits from entering the most sacred part of the shrine. Usually one has its mouth open, the other closed. Two interesting explanations for this I've heard follow: Sometimes it is better to speak wisdom; sometimes it is better to listen to it. Another: One lion-dog holds its mouth in the shape of the first letter of the Japanese alphabet (a = *agyo*) and the other's mouth is in the shape of the last letter (n = *ungyo*). Together they represent the whole universe (alpha and omega). Perhaps by passing between them one enters a place where all things are possible.

Fukuoka is a port city. Boats coming into port signal prosperity.

A Boat Ride in Yanagawa (p. 60):
The boatman was likely singing songs by the famous locally born poet Hakushū Kitahara (1885-1942) whose children's songs, set to music by Kosaku Yamada (1886-1965), are well known throughout Japan. The passengers (all were Japanese but for our small party) undoubtedly recalled them, along with other happy childhood memories.

Gunkanjima (p. 62):
The tiny island of Hashima, also known as Gunkanjima (Battleship Island), is located off the coast of Nagasaki. Formerly a densely populated coal mining community, it

was suddenly abandoned in 1974 after over 80 years of intense productivity. Pummeled by winds and salty sea spray, the buildings and other remaining structures have severely decayed over the years. The island is now a tourist attraction offering guided tours and a virtual museum.

Twenty-six were killed (p. 62):
Twenty Japanese and six foreign born Christians were crucified on Nishizaka Hill in Nagasaki on February 5, 1597. It is currently the site of the Twenty-Six Martyrs Museum and Monument, a Japanese National Sanctuary. Pope John Paul II visited on February 26, 1981, and Pope Francis on November 24, 2019.

Unperturbed, Kannon (p. 63):
Kannon, the bodhisattva of compassion and sorrow, is one of the most popular deities in Japanese Buddhism. In earlier times Kannon (Avalokiteshvara) was male but gradually evolved into a feminine deity (Guanyin in China). She is also identified as the goddess of mercy. A colossal statue of her stands in Nagasaki in the middle of a hillside cemetery on top of a building shaped like a tortoise. In Buddhism the tortoise represents longevity, loyalty, and wisdom.

His last day on earth (p. 63):
Dedicated in 1995, the Reclining Buddha at Nanzoin Temple in Sasaguri is 135 feet long and 36 feet high, one of the largest bronze statues in the world. It depicts Buddha during his last illness just prior to death and his attainment of *parinirvana*. He is lying on his right side with his left hand on his left thigh and his right hand elevating his face, which with closed eyes appears very relaxed and youthful.

Legend has it that after spreading his teaching for decades, Buddha finally came to a place where, in exchange for his lesson, he was offered a meal of tainted food. Not wishing to offend his host, he ate it anyway. He soon became seriously ill and, knowing that he was dying, he instructed his disciples to lay him down on his right side with his head pointing north and his face turned to the setting sun. Significantly, with the Buddha in this position, anyone looking into his face would be facing the rising sun.

APPENDIX

For Robert* (2010)

There are no more such gentle souls as yours.

Infectious peace, unending patience,
hushed voice of kindness still echoes in my ear.
Quiet comfort, steady presence,
deepest well of serenity reflects in mirrored memory.

Anger, contempt, complaint, and regret—
all foreign foes—can find no foothold in your heart.

Unfathomable talent brings use to the useless.
Unfailing industry resolutely treads
the endless paths of invention to serve as much
and as many as the day's hours allow.

---

* The author's father-in-law, Robert Forest Hutton (1921-2010). See p. 84.

No problem hopeless, no request too great,
your presence makes time flow by,
easy and slow,
like warm butter over grits.

No, don't go.
Stay awhile and we'll chat...

We are stronger for your caring,
braver for your calm,
more forgiving for your acceptance of us
just as we are.

BIBLIOGRAPHY

Bashō, Matsuo, *The Narrow Road to the Deep North and Other Travel Sketches,* trans. by Nobuyuki Yuasa. New York: Penguin Books, 1966.

Blyth, Reginald Horace, *Haiku, in Four Volumes (vol 1: Eastern Culture, vol 2: Spring; vol. 3: Summer-Autumn; vol. 4: Autumn-Winter).* Brooklyn, NY: Angelico Press, 2021. (First published by The Hokuseido Press, 1949-1952).

Haiku: An Anthology of Japanese Poems, ed. by Stephen Addiss. Boston: Shambhala Publications, 2009.

Hass, Robert, *The Essential Haiku: Versions of Bashō, Buson, and Issa.* Hopewell, NJ: The Ecco Press, 1994.

Insight Guide: Japan (3rd edition), Stephen Mansfield. Maspeth, NY: Langenscheidt Publishers, Inc., 2003.

Land of the Reed Plains: Ancient Japanese Lyrics from the Manyoshu, ed. and trans. by Kenneth Yasuda. Rutland, VT: Tuttle Publishing, 1972.

Rexroth, Kenneth, *One Hundred Poems from the Chinese.* New York: New Directions Publishing, 1971.

Ross, Bruce, *How to Haiku: A Writer's Guide to Haiku and Related Forms.* Rutland, VT: Tuttle Publishing, 2002.

Sato, Hiroaki, *On Haiku.* New York: New Directions Publishing Co., 2018.

Smith, Harrison, "Pulitzer-winning formalist poet with an eye on rural life," *The Washington Post,* November 24, 2024, C4.

The Sound of Water: Haiku by Bashō, Buson, Issa, and other poets, trans. by Sam Hamill. Boston: Shambhala Publications, 2000.

Wilson, William Scott, *A Beginner's Guide to Japanese Haiku*. Rutland, VT: Tuttle Publishing, 2022.

Yasuda, Kenneth, *The Japanese Haiku*. Rutland VT: Tuttle Publishing, 1957.

Yasuda, Kenneth (Shōson), *A Pepper Pod*. New York: Alfred A. Knopf, 1947.

Websites:

The Haiku Foundation: www.thehaikufoundation.org

The Haiku Society of America: www.hsa-haiku.org

Modern Haiku: www.modernhaiku.org

Films:

The Buddha: The Story of Siddhartha. Directed by David Grubin, PBS Documentary, 2010.

Perfect Days. Directed by Wim Wenders, Master Mind Limited and Spoon, Inc., 2023.

VERA KOCHANOWSKY has maintained an active career as a choral conductor, harpsichord soloist, chamber musician, and private music teacher in the Washington DC area for more than thirty years. Her interest in writing has been lifelong, but *101 Haiku* is her first published poetry collection. Her two previous books were family histories. The first, *Lenin, Hitler, and Me*, is a retelling of her father Boris Kochanowsky's account of his escapes from communist Russia and Nazi Germany. Her second book, *Anna and Boris: The Love Letters (1944-1946)*, a translation of her parents' correspondence in Switzerland during and just after World War II, offers a detailed, personal portrait of both of her parents.

JANINE JOHNSON, artist, harpsichordist, and composer, resides in Berkeley, California. Growing up in Southern California, she studied both piano and art privately and at California State University Northridge. She became interested in the harpsichord as a teenager, and at age fifteen she combined her love of music and art by building her first harpsichord from a kit. Subsequently, she devoted herself to building harpsichords and fortepianos (as Janine Poletti). Since 1986, she has been building and decorating harpsichords with the renowned maker John Phillips. Her recent work can be viewed at www.jph.us.

www.ingramcontent.com/pod-product-compliance
Lightning Source LLC
Chambersburg PA
CBHW040824131025
33931CB00008B/12

* 9 7 9 8 8 8 6 7 9 8 5 8 6 *